CW00557895

Cliff Entwistle has been married to Yvonne for over forty years, and together they have known both the blessing of a growing family and the heartache of lives taken too soon.

Cliff worked as a coal miner for over twenty-five years, and today instructs forklift truck drivers. He has also been a sitting district councillor for Bassetlaw for over eighteen years.

Together with his wife, Cliff enjoys working on his home and garden, and visiting historic sites around the UK. He also writes on various topics and recently has been published in a national magazine.

Dedication

To all the people incarcerated that are innocent.

Clifford Entwistle

NEIL'S STORY: TRIAL BY MEDIA

AUSTIN MACAULEY PUBLISHERS™

LONDON · CAMBRIDGE · NEW YORK · SHARJAH

Copyright © Clifford Entwistle (2018)

The right of Clifford Entwistle to be identified as author of this work has been asserted by him in accordance with section 77 and 78 of the Copyright, Designs and Patents Act 1988.

All rights reserved. No part of this publication may be reproduced, stored in a retrieval system, or transmitted in any form or by any means, electronic, mechanical, photocopying, recording, or otherwise, without the prior permission of the publishers.

Any person who commits any unauthorised act in relation to this publication may be liable to criminal prosecution and civil claims for damages.

A CIP catalogue record for this title is available from the British Library.

ISBN 9781528900577 (Paperback)
ISBN 9781528900584 (E-Book)

www.austinmacauley.com

First Published (2018)
Austin Macauley Publishers Ltd™
25 Canada Square
Canary Wharf
London
E14 5LQ

Table of Content

Introduction

In 2006, my daughter-in-law, Rachel, and my only granddaughter, Lillian Rose, were found dead in their home in Massachusetts. In 2008, my eldest son, Neil, was wrongly convicted of murdering his family. I will outline in this book the key points that show that Neil is innocent. I will show that evidence not only leaves reasonable doubt, as the law requires, but that it actually points to Rachel as the one who fired the gun. I will show that Neil was subjected to a farcical trial fuelled by an incomplete investigation and a highly prejudicial media.

Throughout this case, the authorities were found to have withheld evidence that would have given a precise picture of what happened at the crime scene. For example, it was revealed in trial that forensic evidence was withheld from the medical examiner who did the autopsy by the prosecutors. This evidence would have been instrumental in proving that Rachel was, in fact, the person who fired the gun. The very gunshot residue particles they were desperate to find on Neil or anything he had touched, all to no avail, were found on Rachel, as she was found to have gun-shot residue on both hands front and back. These details were quickly hidden, even from the media. Why?

On the stand during trial, forensic chemists and experienced homicide detectives said that, while at the crime scene following the discovery of Rachel and Lillian's bodies, they did not know how Rachel and Lillian had died. They said this despite the bloodied garments worn by Lillian, garments that were displayed for extended periods during the trial to ensure full emotional effect. Despite their claimed ignorance, they chose to perform no test to determine cause of death, nor did they invite the medical examiner's office to the crime scene. Why? What was being hidden?

When questioned during the trial, a forensic chemist first confirmed that she should indeed enter a crime scene with an open mind and an objective mind-set, yet she reluctantly confirmed that, on leaving the police station, and before entering the house and the crime scene for the first time, she had listed Neil as the main suspect on her form.

Following the deaths of Rachel and Lillian, and the subsequent arrest of Neil, it was constantly reported in the media that Rachel had died first and Lillian after. During the trial, however, it was shown that the opposite was true. The shot that killed Rachel, killed her instantly. Bruising shows that the bullet that killed dear little Lillian passed through her tiny body and entered Rachel's breast while Rachel was still alive. The first shot killed little Lillian. The second shot killed Rachel. Why would the media lie or be fed this lie? Because it fits the story they wished to tell. They needed Neil to be the killer, so they had to say that Rachel died first; otherwise, they would have to explain why she didn't react like a lioness protecting her cub, as indeed would have been the case if Lillian were shot first by another. Of course, by the time the trial arrived, the jurors' ears were closed to anything that contradicted what they had been fed for the previous two-and-a-half years.

Neil's case was run by and through the media. Various police and prosecutorial authorities constantly added fuel by leaking false information and withholding facts. They did this so that any potential jurors would become prejudiced against our innocent son long before the trial began. What chance of a fair trial? Absolutely none!

Our Catastrophic News

Neil was born in 1978 and brought up in a typical working-class family home in Worksop, North Nottinghamshire, England. Neil's mother, Yvonne, is a school cook and I have been a standing District Councillor for eighteen years. Neil also has a younger brother, Russell. After Neil took his A levels at the local comprehensive school, he completed a GAP year at IBM in Warwickshire. Following this, Neil completed a Master's Degree in Electronic Engineering at the University of York and it was at York that Neil met Rachel.

Rachel, a student of English Literature at the College of the Holy Cross in Massachusetts, was attending York as part of her Junior Year Abroad. Neil and Rachel met, became close friends, and eventually, fell in love at the rowing club. For most of the academic year, they were in the same boat together, Neil as stroke, Rachel as coxswain.

After they both graduated in 2002, they got engaged to be married and their wedding took place on the 10th August 2003 in Rachel's hometown of Plymouth, Massachusetts. Following their wedding and honeymoon, they returned to Worcester, England, to set up home. Neil worked for QinetiQ in Malvern and Rachel taught at a high school in Redditch. Within a year, Rachel was pregnant and Lillian Rose entered our lives on the 9th April 2005.

In August of 2005, the family emigrated to the United States. Within a month of Lillian's birth, Rachel had started to show signs of depression and she wanted to be back home with her mother. At the invitation of Rachel's mum and stepfather, Priscilla and Joseph Matterazzo, the new family moved into the Matterazzo's home in Carver, Massachusetts.

Tensions in the house were much greater than any of them had anticipated, however. Rachel shared with us that she was not settling in, that Lillian had stopped sleeping through the night, and that there were constant arguments between herself, Priscilla and Joseph. For the sake of keeping peace, Neil and Rachel decide to move out. They moved into a home in Hopkinton, Massachusetts, around the 10th January 2006.

Within ten days of the family moving into their new home, tragedy struck. Neil was in the kitchen when he heard a loud bang. He immediately ran upstairs to where he believed Rachel and little Lillian to be, and he arrived at the threshold of the master bedroom just as Rachel turned the gun on herself, and fired it a second time. Rachel's eyes met Neil's just before she pulled the trigger; he saw the light go out of them.

Our son went into shock. His mind shut down, and from that point on, a mixture of the shock and his love for Rachel, a desire to protect her still being within him, led to him following a bizarre path of events that make little sense to anyone thinking rationally. After driving around in the family vehicle, which at a later date would be tooth combed for gunshot residue, not a trace of which was found, Neil ended up at the airport. He had witnessed a terrifying and traumatic scene, he had lost his world, and an instinct to be with Mum and Dad led him to fly home.

Neil himself calls it the most miserable inadequate and inexcusable of decisions, but it is accepted in the medical field that viewing such trauma, and such unthinkable horror leads one's mind to become numb in order to protect itself. In trial, the prosecutor stated that Neil had pre-booked the flight home, which was totally untrue. Why would this prosecutor lie? Only one reason: to secure a guilty verdict for an innocent man.

Upon receiving the tragic and catastrophic news about Rachel and dear Lillian, I fell to my knees, and Yvonne went into shock for weeks. We immediately contacted the Matterazzo's.

Were we naïve? Yes. Were we all in shock? Yes. Did these two things lead us to make the very stupid decision of allowing Neil to speak to the police? We had no idea that Neil's words would be later twisted as they were and this twisted form of his words, along with other false information, would be shared in the public forum by both, police and prosecutors, as the initial investigation was still, supposedly, ongoing.

Let me share with you one example: Neil told the US police that, on finding his family the way he had, his thought was to be with them and that he considered taking his own life by using a kitchen knife. The forensic investigators were all over these knives, trying to find gunshot residue particles left on them by Neil, but they found none. This was stated during the trial, but the media reported their source as confirming a positive test for gunshot residue. Where did the media get this information? They use the freedom of press as an excuse for making such false and prejudicial statements, knowing that they cannot be held accountable for their actions. When false statements are fed to the press, who then report it without verification or apology, it becomes a trial run by the media.

In all of this, no one seemed to ask what is to me the obvious question: If Neil had used the gun to commit the crime, why would he then use a knife to kill himself? Surely, with a loaded gun in his hand, he would have turned the gun on himself. In many cases where family members are murdered by another family member, this is what happens. The only explanation as to why Neil stated this is that he didn't use the gun.

We cooperated with the local police who were daily arriving at our home and we even volunteered Neil's passport to them. To better cope with the situation, my wife and I at first did not watch the TV or listen to the radio. We needed time to come to terms with the enormity of the situation. We had not just ourselves to think of, but our aging parents too. This situation called for all our strength and courage; we knew it would break us if we didn't hold strong together. Our belief in our son's innocence has given us the strength to be able to face people and to look them in the eyes. At no time has Neil ever caused me any embarrassment or shame. Even today, upon waking up, the first thought that comes to my mind is that Neil is locked away many miles from his family.

From the beginning, we were inundated by offers from the media outlets in America, including the Larry King show. Martin Bashir, who famously interviewed Michael Jackson and Lady Diana, also wanted to interview us. We declined both offers. As the case broke out, the media satellite vans were camped outside our home for two weeks. If I left the house, I would, rightly or wrongly, ignore the presence of the journalists at the front of our home. They would try to provoke me by the comments they made or by setting off a bright camera flash directly in my face; they were disappointed, however, because I did not give them their desired reaction.

The Dehumanisation of Neil

The District Attorney's office needed to create a motive to support their allegations against Neil. Neil was not going to gain through insurance policies, so that was out. The best they could come up with was that Neil had money troubles, even though he had just paid three month's rent money in advance. They tried to support this with the claim that Neil was unemployed, but it was agreed in trial that Neil was seeking employment and that a company was trying to get hold of him through messages left on the Matterazzo's answering machine. Besides, if Neil's finances were in such dire straits, he would have asked us for help; we own our house outright and we both have stable jobs.

As for evidence, they claimed that Neil's DNA was on the butt of the murder weapon and yet, the owner of the gun, Rachel's stepfather, said he had previously taken Neil to a gun club for target practice with the very weapon. Until the trial was in session, it was not disclosed that the only person to have a fingerprint on the trigger of the weapon was Rachel's stepfather himself. This was not disclosed in the extradition papers. We believe this was omitted so that the British government would not start asking questions, but as I shall show later, it is unlikely they would anyway. It was also claimed that the house laptop was used to find ways to kill and yet, in trial it was proven that no DNA or fingerprint testing had ever been done on it to prove who had used it. Why? Only days before the killings, this laptop had been in the Matterazzo's household where Rachel and Neil had been living, and it was available for anyone to use. The password was known to all: the name of Rachel and Neil's dog. Even we knew it. When the defence lawyer stated this, he held the laptop up in the palm of his hand in the courtroom.

This, though, did not stop the authorities from condemning Neil to the media, who then attacked Neil relentlessly. They set out to get Neil convicted by releasing extensive misleading and unsubstantiated information to the press in general. They worked on the basis that if someone is told something often enough, they will eventually believe it and thus, it would be easier to get the conviction they wanted. What the authorities recognise is that most people believe what they read in the newspapers and what they watch on the TV. These attacks on Neil were one way traffic and we, as a family, were not in a position to hit back.

Too soon, the authorities had decided that Neil was their only suspect. Having decided that, they rushed into the investigation. On the 10th February 2006, at a press conference, the District Attorney's office released details of their investigation into the case. Four days later, a court allowed 200 pages of documents to be allowed into the public domain. At this point, alibis of people involved in the case had not yet even been completed, but then Neil was their only target. Information released included personal data found on the family home laptop computer, along with details of items found in the home and the car of the family. Also included was a two-hour conversation that took place without respite, that Neil had with the American police from our home.

In a local Massachusetts newspaper on the 8th February 2006, it was stated that the Middlesex District Attorney's Office rejected a public information request from a local newspaper to obtain copies or transcripts of telephone calls between Rachel and her mother just before the crime had been committed. This could have given people an idea of Rachel's state of mind at the time, but if this had been to the detriment of Neil, it would have surely been released. When the failure to release this information was challenged, it was rejected because it was said that it could jeopardise the State's case! Another case of working very hush, hush by the authorities, when it suits.

Whilst the more respectable media outlets no doubt tried to retain some impartiality, they were nevertheless guilty of reporting on information put out into the public domain by the District Attorney's Office. When an accusation was made against Neil, without foundation or proof to back it up, the word allegedly was rarely used, such was the ferocity of their frenzied attack. The scale of these horrific one-way media attacks on Neil, and the likelihood that Rachel and Lillian's funeral would be turned into a media circus, led to Neil's heart-breaking decision not to attend the funeral. I was with Neil in his lawyer's office in London, when his lawyer advised against it. In fact, he stated that the press would be watching for the moment to take a photo shot of Neil, which would make it look as if he were either smiling or enjoying himself. This was good advice, as this is exactly what happened in trial, when photographs of Rachel and Lillian were shown of the crime scene in the courtroom. Images such as this were used in a TV programme that went out on Channel 5 titled 'Witness: Smile of a killer.' Even a British forensic psychologist, one who has never met Neil, stated in the programme that Neil was amused at what he was seeing with the jurors. Obviously, these were complete and utter lies, but it just shows you what some people will do to get on the TV.

Promotions and commendations were going to be gained from this case if they could get Neil convicted, and they were not going to let an opportunity like this go. The American authorities knew that this British subject would not be protected by his own government, as all the British were interested in was pleasing the Americans, as indeed proved to be the case. The British government have been our undoing and they proved to be the enemy within, when they allowed the Americans to have access to our telephones lines. What Neil's grandfather would think of the actions of the British government against his grandson, I don't know. My father was in the Royal Engineers and was at the Battle of Dunkirk like thousands of other soldiers surrounded by the Germans in May of 1940, and my mother served in the ATS in WWII.

Like millions of others, these people thought that they were doing their best for the benefit of their country and this is their reward.

Who Said What

At the very beginning, an ex-homicide investigator with the state police was the spokesperson for Rachel's family. This person, who was now running a private law business, was at the forefront in the media making unreserved attacks on Neil, accusing him of betraying Rachel's family. He was on the most famous chat shows in the US, the Larry King show and the Anderson Cooper 360 degrees show, talking about the case. This spokesman was involved in directing the police in the case, even before the bodies were found. Why? According to a book published and released at the start of the trial, which was titled 'Heartless: The True Story of Neil Entwistle And The Cold Blooded Murder of his Wife And Child', he requested the police call a particular detective in on his day off, to take the job on from start to finish, which he did. We found it strange that this civilian was controlling the police. Was this not outside his jurisdiction?

In September 2008, it was reported in the Boston Globe that the spokesperson for the Matterazzo's was piloting his boat when someone unexplainably fell off it and drowned. It was reported by the Globe that they could not reach this spokesperson following the incident on his law phone or his cell phone. This spokesman who was quite willing to destroy my family as he helped to ensure that Neil did not get a fair trial, makes himself scarce and all of a sudden has no comments to make. A witness on board stated that the owner of the boat and the deceased had probably had drinks on the boat. When the deceased was later found washed up, the toxicologist's report stated that there was alcohol found within his body. A decision was made by the police not to breathalyse the owner and pilot of the boat, according to the Globe. Why? This would be normal procedure to breathalyse someone in this situation otherwise why would the Globe state this fact, what would have been its relevance.

This spokesman for the Matterazzo's went on major TV shows and stated, 'All we need now is the right jury pool.' What was the right jury pool? Would it be one that was in the State that Neil was in, as the judge was not going to allow it to be taken out of that State? Was also the right jury pool one that was tainted, brainwashed and misled by what was being put out in the media daily? Yes, this was the right jury pool they were after. What would have been the wrong jury pool? One that would have been allowed to have made their own mind up, based on facts, looked at it objectively and picked up on GSR on Rachel's hands being withheld from the medical examiner.

On the steps of the courthouse whilst the trial was in progress, I made a statement to the cameras and said that when the spokesperson for Rachel's family stated in the media, "All we need now is the right jury pool." I knew from this point that Neil was not going to receive a fair trial, which proved to be the case.

In the book published before trial, it is stated on pages 178 -179: "they had the court of public opinion, which had already convicted the guy." The burden was now on the defence to convince people of Neil's innocence. Presumption of innocence was now void. The use of the media by the District Attorney's office and the media's willingness to be used, had proved to be most effective. The trial to come was a mere formality and Neil's defence could do nothing to change that.

This author of the book was reported in the Boston Globe in September 2015, to have been charged with assaulting a police officer and with resisting arrest. This author who was trying to make money by publishing a book at the time of the trail on the back of Rachel and Lillian's death. Feeding information into the public domain to ensure that Neil would not receive a fair trial.

It was agreed in trial that, when the police were trying to locate Neil and his family, they never thought to phone us. When asked why, they said that they did not have our telephone number!

In the Boston Globe only a few weeks after the bodies were found, a quote was made from the District Attorney's Office that Neil Entwistle had committed the murders but then failed to commit suicide. It was said that Entwistle first shot his wife through the head and then shot his daughter through the abdomen. I am disgusted by those who seem to relish in the tragedy that has befallen my family, especially when the details are in regard to my granddaughter. The author seems to delight in the gruesome details and writes in chapter 9: "Rachel had died instantly from the shot to her head, but the bullet hurtled through the baby's stomach had worked more slowly, meaning that little Lillian had suffered in pain spooned to her mother's body." Their perverse delight in the macabre details aside, where was their proof? They did not even use the word allegedly. As I have stated previously, the reverse happened due to the fact that the bruising around the wound in Rachel's left breast proved to be a non-fatal shot and that her heart must have still been beating at this point, before the fatal shot to her head. The truth was disclosed in trial, but it was too late to have any effect on a public and jury, who had heard and believed the reverse for over two years.

A US defence lawyer of Neil's, on British television, said that Rachel was the shooter, given the evidence available, and that in our society, suicide is often taboo and is considered by many to be shameful. Suicide tarnishes the memory of a loved one, and it leaves friends and family questioning themselves. They may ask what signs did I miss and is there anything I could have done to prevent this. In the UK, one in ten women get post-natal depression before their child gets to one year old (NHS figures) and the thought of hurting their child comes into the top band of things that are a likely occurrence from this condition. In the US, studies proved that in suicide cases, handguns were the preferred weapon. Ninety-two percent of women who commit suicides use handguns and seventy-two percent of women shoot themselves in the head. When people shoot themselves, they do not necessarily hold the weapon the same way they would as if firing at a target. Rachel was not checked to see if she was suffering from a history of post-partum depression. This condition is too common in new mothers to be overlooked. So is the fact that more women commit suicide with a firearm each year in the US than are intentionally killed by another person with one. According to The World Almanac and Book of Facts 2011, quoting the 2006 data from the National Safety Council, 2,149 females in the US committed suicide using a firearm in 2006, compared to 1,905 females who were intentionally killed by another person using one. Despite these figures, wrong though they are by at least a count of one for that year, they had no effect on the forensic investigator who, before entering the house and crime scene in Hopkinton, had listed murder on her form for the cause of Rachel's death and had listed Neil as the main suspect.

A leading US forensic psychiatrist, who wrote a landmark 1969 study, stated that mothers are the most likely to kill a newly born baby, because of mental illness such as post-partum depression or because they can't handle the stress of caring for a baby.

A District Attorney's Office spokesperson, when they were questioned about why the police had gone into Neil's home by breaking in when there was no sign of an emergency, stated that the police wanted to see if there was a smell of carbon monoxide gas within the house. Wouldn't this be the job of the fire department, said Neil's defence lawyer. Needless to say, carbon monoxide has no smell!

London Beckons

In February 2006, Neil and I volunteered to be driven to the American Embassy in London. We were escorted in a car by two British police officers and we intended to meet with the American police in the embassy, as was publicised in the media. First, we agreed to make a detour in London to see a lawyer before arriving at the embassy. Neil's lawyer advised us not to make the rendezvous and we were also warned that our telephones could be tapped into. How right he was.

In comparison to the way that Rachel's family were treated by their government representatives, here we had our government setting us up to go into the lion's den unprotected. Luckily, I got advice not to trust this situation without seeing a legal expert first.

Eventually, the American's had the authority to have Neil arrested, which was in London when Neil was with friends. The reason Neil had gone to London was he thought to take the media away from our house. Neil was intercepted by the Metropolitan police whilst using the tube.

As Neil was to appear at Bow Street Court, to face the very real prospect of being extradited, I was to meet Neil's London barrister and lawyer inside the building. I travelled on my own to London and I made sure that I was there early. I remember going into Starbucks just around the corner from the courthouse, to pass on a little time. On approach to the courthouse, it was clear to see that the media presence had already built up, although I remember entering the building without too much trouble.

Prior to travelling to London, I was told by Neil's legal team that they wanted to fight the extradition and apply for bail. I was told to make financial provision for this, but when I arrived, they had changed their minds and were going to get Neil to volunteer to be extradited.

Neil's legal team informed me that under the Extradition Act 2003, Neil could not be extradited to a state that had the death penalty; Massachusetts did not. This was certainly something you would not forget being said to you. I was told that I was dealing with the situation well, as usually the people they represent, give them a hard time by continually moaning about the situation they find themselves in. Neil was only in court a few minutes. We glanced at each other and Neil briefly nodded at me. My heart broke as this was my son. I cannot describe how I felt; I do not know which words to use. I was deflated, for Neil, Yvonne, Russell and myself. How were we going to cope? Once as I looked across the courtroom, I caught the look of what appeared to be a blonde female journalist and I will never forget the look of glee on her face as she looked directly at me. She had no concern for the situation my family was in.

When the court session finished, due to all the media attention at the front of the courthouse, I was led out to the rear of the building. Neil's lawyer went out to speak to the press and stated; 'Neil believes he will have a fair and proper hearing in the US. Neil has consented at the earliest opportunity because he wants to co-operate with the authorities in any way that he can. He is anxious his delay might cause his wife's family and his own, additional stress.' Neil could leave the UK in a matter of days.

On the same day that Neil was to be extradited, I had the opportunity to visit him in Her Majesty's Prison, Pentonville, London. If it had not been for the intervention of Neil's lawyers, this meeting would not have taken place. Trying to organise an appointment to be able to visit Neil before leaving home, even using two telephones simultaneously, was impossible. We were trying for hours to get through on the prison answering system, but with no success.

When I arrived at the prison and was eventually able to see Neil, I was with him for just over an hour before the guards came to take him away for his transfer to the US. At this meeting, I had a message from Neil's lawyer which was for Neil to speak to no one on the flight. On this visit, emotions did get the better of me and I broke down.

When I left the prison, my intention was to go straight home and my journey started from Kings Cross railway station. As I arrived on the station platform, on a massive overhead TV screen was a photographic image of Neil, Rachel and Lillian together as a family. How thankful I was that my wife Yvonne had not travelled with me to be subjected to this.

On the 9th February 2006 at 1425 hrs, we had our home searched by the Metropolitan Police and there was no warning that these four police officers were going to go through our home. It was well publicised by the media afterwards, as they were still holding vigil outside our home. This search was conducted under the Extradition Act of 2003, and the search was conducted mainly in Neil's bedroom and our house computers were confiscated.

At a later stage, I mentioned to our local beat bobby that our police seemed to treat us fairly. He said to me that that was only because you have cooperated.

Neil's Extradition

Neil was driven out to Gatwick airport to be extradited in an unmarked car, and he was handed over to ten US Marshals who searched, cuffed and chained him on the runway. He was then led up the steps in this way, into a private chartered aeroplane; the cost to the US tax payer was a million dollars. Neil was sat for eight hours, where he could not move an inch, and the Marshals offered him a sandwich and a drink with a grin. He was also shown the latest copy of the American magazine 'People,' where the front cover bore a photograph with Neil, Rachel and Lillian on it, with the caption, 'Who killed Rachel and her baby?'

Neil was questioned illegally on this flight, according to Neil's defence lawyers. Here, the defence lawyers were making sure that any evidence that the authorities thought they had and could be used against Neil by questioning him on the flight, was not allowed as evidence in trial. It was proven that the statements were not voluntary given, but rather obtained in violation of his rights. The critical factor was that the Marshals did not electronically record by tape the conversations or let Neil review their notes for accuracy. Neil had the right to remain silent and to be free from unwanted custodial interrogation.

That, the British government allowed my son to be handed over to the Marshals in this way, really disgusts me. I challenged the Home Office and asked why Neil was not allowed at least an independent witness or legal representative on the flight. Their answer was that there was no provision in the Extradition Act to warrant this. Then, in one reply from a government minister, it was stated that Neil should have asked the Marshals for this support! Then why weren't we told this? Why were we kept in the dark? I approached the Parliamentary Ombudsman to look into this, but they said that it was outside their jurisdiction.

There was a massive presence of media personnel waiting for Neil to exit the aircraft on American soil. When Neil emerged from the aircraft on the military air base, he was led out in shackles. Neil told me that he was so tightly trussed up that it made him stoop as he tried to walk. All the TV channels, within the area of Massachusetts, were immediately broken into, and these images were broadcast live and were repeated for days after that. This spectacle was, of course, staged by the authorities to taint the potential jury, who could only come to one decision on Neil's guilt when observing these images.

Who sanctioned the authorisation for the civilian helicopters, which were holding media personnel, to be in this military airspace? How high would this kind of authorisation have had to have come from? Only the arrival of such as, the President of the United States, would have been allowed this kind of authorisation. Neil's defence lawyer said, "I am certain anybody watching this telecast has already formed an opinion of Neil's guilt. There should never be a case ever, where the media does nothing but stage an event to the detriment of the accused's opportunity to a fair trial."

The Enemy Within

At about the same period, we finally had the proof that our telephone conversations were being listened into. When putting the hand set down following a local call, we heard American voices as if in a call centre, but before this we heard a lot of clicking on the line. We immediately informed Neil's legal team of this and this activity was soon stopped. They said at the time that the authorities must have gone through the US courts to get permission to do this. As far as we know, we never had another similar occasion. It also seemed that the British government had played their part here in allowing this tapping to take place. Such electronic surveillance conducted in the UK is governed solely by UK law, even if requested by the US.

This was put on a back burner at the time because we had plenty of other matters to deal with. Eventually, I contacted the Foreign Office with regards to the issue and I was told to get in touch with Independent Police Complaints Commission, which was the wrong department. A different angle was needed and so, I sent a letter to the Prime Minister's Office. Finally, we received a letter from the Home Secretary, Theresa May, who said that she was answering on behalf of the Prime Minister. She stated that the lawful interception can be carried out in the UK, by a limited number of specified public authorities, under the authorisation of a warrant issued by the Secretary of State. A warrant can only be issued, if it is necessary in the interest of national security, for the purposes of safeguarding the economic wellbeing of the United Kingdom.

The letter went on to say that there is no power to issue a warrant for interception to be carried out in the UK by the authorities of another country. However, the Secretary of State may agree to issue a warrant for interception to be carried out of another country, but only if it satisfies the condition I have described. It is important to note that intentional interception without lawful authority is a criminal offence.

The letter concluded by saying that "the Independent Investigatory Powers Tribunal can investigate anything you believe has taken place against you, in relation to the interception of communications by public authorities. I hope that this letter goes someway to address your concerns. A copy of this letter will be sent to the Prime Minister."

Following this letter, I did contact the IPT who said that we were out of time with the application and even after we appealed this decision, they said that they would not investigate our complaint.

Extradition Treaty 2003

David Cameron stated, prior to the 2010 general election, that if the Conservatives got in power, they would be reviewing the Extradition Treaty 2003 between the UK and US, as it was too much in favour of the Americans. As the new coalition government was formed in 2010, this is what they set out to do. Our Home Secretary said that they would be reviewing five key areas. One of those was whether the requesting state should be made to provide, upon examination, prima facie evidence, sufficient corroborating evidence to exist to support a case and also to give the Home Secretary powers to stop any extradition.

I informed the government of our own concerns given our experiences and we had the perfect opportunity to do this, since part of the review included a provision where the general public could put their opinions to the panel. Sir Scott Baker was leading the review and the closing date was in December 2010. The panel was expected to report back to the government by late summer in 2011. The eventual conclusion of the independent review found no reason to believe that it was operating unfairly, a decision being studied by the Home Secretary.

In 2010, prior to the election victory of the Conservative party, a letter was sent by me to question the extradition process. Replies were sent back from their office, and they stated the letter would go in front of David Cameron MP, William Hague MP and Dominic Grieve QC MP of the Shadow Justice and the Foreign Affairs team, which was telling me that we had an argument to make.

Critics of the treaty say it is much easier to extradite people from the UK than from the US because the US does not need to present evidence to a British court to request an extradition. Conversely, the UK must first provide sufficient evidence to establish possible cause. The treaty, as it stands, was originally designed to help bring terrorist suspects to justice, but campaigners say it is being used for other offences, such as fraud and drug-trafficking. Between 2003 and 2009, there were 63 extraditions to the US from the UK, and only one was for terrorist activities. An enquiry in 2014 by the House of Lords asked whether it protects suspects who ought to be considered innocent until proven guilty.

We took the step to inform Neil that he had to give his permission for his London based lawyers to release his extradition papers to us, which he did. We were more than a little surprised by the content of these papers, given that Neil's liberty was taken away based on what was said.

In the extradition papers, a reference was made to a match of Neil's DNA being on the butt of the gun involved in the case. Yet, no oral swab had been taken from Neil. According to Neil's defence lawyer, this made the claim unreliable and violated Neil's rights to a fair trial.

In an affidavit in September 2006, a supervisor with the Massachusetts Department of State Police laboratory stated that, in order for DNA analysis to be reliable, a DNA sample should be taken directly from the suspect or defendant, according with laboratory policy guidelines.

Following the deaths of Rachel and Lillian, the gun was used at Joseph Matterazzo's gun club, following which it was cleaned, according to trial records. Yet, it was stated that Neil's DNA was the most prominent on the butt of the gun. This sounds too convenient to be true. I wonder: Was Neil's DNA on the gun the transferable kind or not?

After Neil had been extradited, the US authorities wanted to take a DNA test from Neil! Up to this point, the word 'match' had been used by the authorities some twenty times in the media, which was of course a false claim. Neil's defence lawyers wanted to challenge this test being done, but were overruled by a judge.

We put all these points to our Home Office, but they said that it was not for a British judge to test the sufficiency of the evidence.

It was stated in the extradition papers that Neil's version of how he found the crime scene did not match that of the investigators. What the authorities failed to say was that the police let civilians into the house when they searched it the first time and they did not find anything. The day after the civilians broke in with a neighbour, they went upstairs in the house and found nothing. Later, the police again broke into the house without a search warrant. In the extradition papers, it states that the investigators, on discovering the bodies, pulled back a pillow covering Lillian's face. On the stand in trial, the investigator said that, as he moved to the top of the bed, he pulled back a comforter before he first observed a baby's face! A question has to be asked about the young family dog that was in the house all the time, but never mentioned, even though it was a basset hound, only second to a bloodhound for its sense of smell!

Gary McKinnon, who, like Neil, was to be extradited to the US, was waiting to see what the future held for him. Gary has a medical condition called Asperger's Syndrome and he was threatening to take his own life if extradited. Gary was facing charges of unauthorised access, from his home computer in London, to 97 US government computers. The systems into which he is said to have hacked included US Army, Navy and NASA computers which were concerned with national defence and security. With the knowledge of how Neil had been treated in custody, we thought that it was our public duty to inform our government of what we knew.

From January 2007, for eighteen months, Neil's cell lights were never turned off, day or night and this is a known CIA torture method used to cause someone sleep deprivation. He was only given an egg sandwich for breakfast, and for lunch throughout this period, two bologna (luncheon meat) and cheese sandwiches. He received no hot food whatsoever. He wore a one piece padded suit, whatever the temperature. Would our Home Secretary have signed Neil's extradition agreement, if he had known that Neil was going to be treated in this way? This was under a one-hundred-year extradition agreement that is based mainly on trust.

Neil personally wrote to the Home Secretary, Theresa May, to let her know of his own experiences and what he thought Gary McKinnon would be subjected to if extradited.

***

Neil's Letter to Theresa May

I wish to make it clear that I have no idea or regard for Mr McKinnon's guilt or innocence, nor do I elicit your help or sympathy for my own cause. I am writing simply to make you aware of how the current extradition treaty with the US fails to protect UK citizens and how it is exploited by the US authorities.

Mr McKinnon will not receive a fair trial. He will be tried by the media, without regard for the circumstances leading to the alleged offence. He will be subjected to a farce of a trial, a trial by a jury who will be prejudiced by the personal attack the media level at him. The US prosecutors are very effective in their exploitation of the media to help convict even those who may be innocent of the charges against them. The judges in the US are both unwilling, and in many ways powerless, to control and limit the effects of such negative, prejudicial publicity.

Mr McKinnon will be interrogated on his flight from the UK by the US Marshals. He will be heavily shackled, cuffed and chained throughout the long journey, with no ability to move whatsoever. The US Marshals will bombard him with questions and whether or not he speaks to them, they will write detailed reports of his supposed conversation with them. They may well use so-called truth drugs to loosen his tongue. At the end of his long flight, he will be paraded before a mass media, portrayed as a vicious criminal with a dazed look, before being forced into a police cruiser for transport to a police station. Once there, he will be further questioned, while they slowly take his fingerprints. At no point will he have legal representatives, or any other protection.

While awaiting trial, Mr McKinnon will be subjected to living conditions that may seriously affect his health. Am I right in believing that Mr McKinnon has some form of mental illness or physical disability? He will be subjected to over twenty-three-and-a-half hours a day in a six-by-four-foot cell. His cell light will burn brightly twenty-four hours daily which, without any complementing sunlight, will confuse his body clock. He will be naked apart from a plastic padded sheet and his cell will be clear of furnishings except for a plastic mattress. Despite having no sunlight, he will be exposed to the winter and summer elements due to open windows at the end of his line of cells, without relief of heating or cool ventilation. All this will be covered by supposed suicide prevention measures, a very convenient loophole used to great effect. You need to be sure that Mr McKinnon can endure such conditions and possibly worse, before you hand him over.

I ask, before you make any decision regarding Mr McKinnon, that you demand much more information about his alleged offences than the current extradition treaty requires. My experience has shown that the US authorities are happy to exploit the fact that the UK does not currently require them to prove the validity of any evidence that they say they have. They can and will lie. Please demand more of them than their word.

*****

In answer, our Home Office stated that, 'we note the subsequent events in the USA, the prison regime there and even the safety of the US conviction. Those, however, are matters which you would need to pursue directly with the US authorities. We can neither assist, nor intervene.'

In 2011, the President of the United States, Mr Obama, visited the UK on a state visit. On the 25th May, the BBC reported that the President said he would respect the British legal process when it came to the position of Mr McKinnon. The Prime Minister, David Cameron, said that the Home

Secretary has to make the final decision as to whether Mr McKinnon is extradited, but said that he understood the widespread concern about the way he would be treated if handed over to the US authorities.

The Home Secretary decided not to allow the extradition of Gary, which was a decision supported by Nick Clegg, the Deputy Prime Minister and Boris Johnson, the Mayor of London. The day before this announcement, we received an email from the Home Office to ask my permission to allow them to publish on their web page our findings that went forward to the Extradition Review. This I did, and it went alongside the top eleven other pieces of work that went towards the enquiry, two from Members of Parliament, one from a Member of the European Union and a further one from a Member of the Queens Council.

Theresa May also said that she was going to make sweeping reforms to the lopsided Extradition Act, to put in place a 'forum bar,' which means more suspects are likely to face trial in the UK, if being suspected of committing a crime in the US, instead of being extradited.

US Lawyer in London

In June of 2006, my wife and I, and our youngest son met Neil's US defence lawyer in London. He was there to meet Neil's London lawyer. We sat in a hotel lobby in a quiet spot to discuss the case. At this meeting, it was agreed to put our house up for Neil's bail money, as the lawyer was going to ask for Neil's bail in the US courts. This was the extent that we were willing to go to, to fight for Neil. Anyway, Neil, he said, had no prior criminal record and posed no danger to anyone if released. Bail was refused by the judge, even though the lawyer mentioned that Neil could be electronically tagged and a global positioning device could track his movements.

In December 2006, we received an urgent message from Neil's US lawyer. This urgency to contact us was because there had been an incident involving Neil at the jail and he didn't want us to get this news second-hand through the media.

The authorities said that Neil had written a suicide letter and this had been uncovered by the prison guards. Officers at the jail said that Neil had written to us and his lawyers to say that he was depressed, and was contemplating taking his own life. Neil was sent to a State Hospital for mental evaluation, but was quickly sent back because there was nothing wrong with him. The hospital said that they were wasting their time. Neil was now put under suicide watch, which was a perfect opportunity for them now to abuse our son.

On Neil's journey to be evaluated at the State Hospital, he only had to wear what he described as a Fred Flintstone outfit in freezing cold weather. Through the forty-four mile journey, he was cuffed, shackled and chained. His bare feet were frozen to the metal floor of the van and only his violent shivering gave him any comfort, as he was perched on a metal bench, trying to remain upright as the van turned corners. The heating could have been put on in the van, but wasn't.

At a later stage, the Sheriff said to the media that Neil never actually threatened to kill himself, but said that he thought he showed tell-tale signs of depression. With regards to Neil's treatment, there should have been a 'Presumption of Innocence' by the Sheriff's department, but, after all, they saw and read the same slanderous reports as everyone else, day after day.

Pre-Trial Visit to the United States

In the Easter period of 2008, we visited Neil for the first time since his extradition to the US. Neil was held in Cambridge on the edge of Boston and before travelling, we made sure that we had a lawyer in place, in case we needed one. We did not know what we were going to be subjected to from the police or the media. We actually ended up leaving the US without the press ever knowing that we had been.

On our visit, we went to the resting place of Rachel and Lilly; we took some white roses, thankful no one else was around. It was a very emotional experience. At the time, we were unaware of the potential danger we were in. It was still a few months before the book 'Heartless' was released, in which the author shares on page 242 that, "Joseph Matterazzo privately said he would stand there with one of his weapons before he would let anyone near the gravesite from the Neil Entwistle's camp." On subsequent visits, this threat was considered so serious by our Foreign and Commonwealth Office that they advised us to notify the State Police if we were visiting. They even told us to consider hiring private security. We also wondered if we were at risk from others in their family. It was told in trial that it was general knowledge that the keys to the guns and ammunition were left out on the kitchen top. However, fearful for our lives, once we learnt of this, Yvonne said to me that Joseph Matterazzo would have to pull the trigger to stop her from going to Rachel and Lilly's grave.

We were invited to the British Consulate in Boston, where we were told by the Vice Consul that Neil would spend the rest of his days in the US if convicted. If Neil were to be transferred to the UK, then the US would have to be the first to start off this process and then it would require our government to agree. Given that our system is more lenient than the American one, we were told that this wasn't very likely to happen. Our Foreign Office visited Neil once in five years, because of the financial restraints they said. They said that Neil could telephone them, but, of course, this would be monitored.

Our hotel was only a five-minute walk from the jail, which was a monstrosity of a building. Neil was kept on the twentieth floor and according to the press, the place stank which wasn't the case. Neil had no idea that we were visiting him and so it must have been quite a surprise since it had been two years since we had seen each other. He thought that it was his lawyers visiting him. It was a very emotional visit and we would not have travelled without first having the clearance from Neil's lawyers. We were facing Neil through a glass partition and we had to hold telephone handsets to communicate.

On one occasion, when we were waiting outside the prison waiting for our eighty-year old cab driver, Ernie, a prison officer came over for a chat. He was telling us about how the old people living locally have to wear outdoor jackets to keep warm inside their houses in winter.

The Trial

In June 2008, myself, Yvonne and Russell landed in Boston for the trial. Again, we did not know what to expect and I was worried about the unknown when it came to my family's security. Were people going to be hostile to us, like they had been to Neil? We had already lost two family members.

Our accommodation was just across the road from the courthouse. We were self-catering, which suited us as we did not want to be seen out any more than we had to. It was our job to take clean shirts in for Neil everyday as we walked into the courthouse, we had to pass the media cameras everyday positioned at the front entrance.

When we arrived on the first day, pandemonium broke out as the press did not know we were going to arrive. As we came out, they were waiting for us, and basically chased us down the street, pushing microphones into our faces and throwing questions at us to get a sound bite. To say that this was uncomfortable for us is an understatement. The only way to remedy this was to give a statement to the cameras, which I did.

Neil's lawyer said to me, "I will give you some advice that I was given, and that is to say what you need to say and then make your exit," and it worked.

Whilst in the courtroom, we were approached by a journalist from 'People' magazine, but we declined their offer of doing an interview.

On one occasion, when walking back to the hotel after a day in court, we were approached from behind. I could hear voices in the distance and eventually, the voices got louder. I thought it was the press, but still I turned to face two men in suits. They were the State Police and wanted to question me. I told them that they would have to go through our lawyer first. This, they said, they would do and we never heard anymore from them. By getting into conversation with them, especially the longer that conversation lasted, would have weakened our basic rights.

In trial, first of all, we went through the jury selection process, where 260 people were scrutinised to see if they were eligible, until the final 16 were selected. Due to all the pre-trial publicity, Neil's lawyer asked the judge for a change of venue, but this was denied. The lawyer also asked that a questionnaire expert be brought in to sift out the potential biased jurors. Again, this request was denied. The same result came when the lawyer asked that the jurors should have a site visit. To see the diagrams of the house layout put up on the wall of the courtroom, is no substitute for a site visit. Cameras were allowed to be used by the media in the courtroom whilst the court was in session and I would find them continually being pointed at my family. Somewhere, at the same time, would be a panel of legal experts watching and observing what was being said in the trial and making comments on the progress to viewers, and this would be going out live.

We would meet the Matterazzo family in the courtroom and in the corridor as we were taking breaks in the proceedings. There was no way our heads would be down. In trial, the Matterazzo family spoke against Neil, but only because they did not want the shame of being labelled as the parents of someone who committed infanticide and the stigma that goes with it.

In the restroom on one occasion, I found myself going in there at the same time as Neil's lawyer and he said to me this is one place you do not talk about the case. The defence lawyer on a lot of occasions would go up to the judge at the start of the day and show the front page of the local newspaper to her, to show the way Neil was being portrayed on a daily basis. The captions to the full-page picture would be degrading Neil. These were on sale just across the road from the courthouse and the jurors were allowed to go home every day.

The prosecutors used the tactics of overburdening the defence by the amount of paper work that they would give to them. They would bury deep any slight changes in their information and the defence would have to go through everything to make sure they did not miss anything.

For Neil's defence, an expert should have explained to the jury why it was not that unusual for someone like Neil to leave the crime scene in the way he did. Things are never what they seem, as the defence lawyer said to the jury in his opening statement.

The Medical Examiner admitted on the stand in trial that he was not aware of the gunshot residue evidence that was on both Rachel's hands, front and back, a clear indicator that this person had fired the gun, but he admitted that he would have wanted this information. Neil's defence team said that this evidence could have been supplied by the District Attorney's Office, the Prosecution or the State Police. We want to know why this evidence wasn't supplied. This could have been the starting point to look at someone else as the shooter and not Neil. Body language was something worth observing. Had the cameras not been so focused on Neil and us in trial, they would have seen the looks of dismay from those who were found to be responsible for this information being withheld, and that these people were visibly sinking into their chairs as if to hide.

When you add to this, the fact that no medical checks were done on Rachel to see if she was suffering from post partem depression, it speaks volumes, but then again, Neil was their only suspect.

When a forensic chemist was on the stand and answering to the defence lawyer, she had to admit that she should go to the crime scene with an open mind. After having just left the police station to go to the crime scene, she agreed that she already had Neil's name down on her paper work as being the main suspect.

Even though very experienced police investigators and forensic chemists were at the crime scene, they agreed that they did not know how Rachel and Lillian had died. They could have, at this point, brought in the person who was going to do the autopsy, the Medical Examiner, but they didn't. If it had been determined at this point that gun shots were fired, then trajectory tests could have been done and these would have been done by the medical examiner's office. These trajectory tests would have shown the line of fire and could have presented a clear picture as to what actually happened, but then again, Neil was their only target.

It was agreed in trial that occult blood tests were not done in the en-suite bathroom of the master bedroom or that the sink plug hole was checked, which is standard practice.

It was proven in trial that Lillian was shot first. If anyone other than Rachel had fired the gun, then Rachel would have been shot first. Before the trial, the District Attorney's office had always stated that Rachel was shot first as it fitted their story that Neil was the shooter.

In trial, it was agreed that text messages were sent between Rachel and her best friend before the crime was committed. When on the stand in trial, this best friend was told by the prosecutor not to disclose the contents of the texts between herself and Rachel. If the contents of these texts had shown that Neil was the threat, then the contents would most definitely have been brought into court. What was in these texts messages that made this friend and her sister sit outside the house of Neil and Rachel's all night in their car, in freezing January weather conditions? Had Rachel told them what she was about to do? Is this why the contents were never disclosed in trial? To the present day, no one knows the content of these texts.

Likewise, a telephone conversation between Rachel and her mum was also never disclosed, even though the media wanted it.

When the forensic people in trial put their hands on the gun involved in the case, they wore gloves so that they did not contaminate it. At a later stage, it may have been required to be retested for DNA or fingerprints. In the closing argument, the prosecutor handled it without gloves on and it even went into the deliberation room for everyone to handle.

As the verdict was given and Neil was found guilty, we were already feeling numb. How the jury could say that it was beyond reasonable doubt that Neil did the deed, I do not know. Perhaps, they would have been in trouble themselves if they had not convicted Neil, such was the hype built up over the case by the authorities.

Following the verdict, Neil's trial lawyers made a statement where they felt that there were very significant issues of constitutional law that were violated in trial and these would go forward to appeal. They were confident of a successful review in the Supreme Court, given that the police made two unlawful entries to Neil's home.

We did get the chance to see Neil before we came home, which was a difficult time for everyone. How could we leave the USA without him? How could we leave our innocent son, who had just been convicted of a crime he did not commit? Yvonne refused to leave, and I pleaded with her at the time and more or less had to drag her to the airport. On the seven-hour flight back home, neither myself, Yvonne nor Russell spoke. Our family had been torn into pieces. We were exhausted. We did not even know which prison Neil would be put long term.

Back Home

When we arrived home from the trial, waiting for us was a bouquet of flowers and attached to them a card from the 'This Morning' programme, signed by Philip Schofield who presented the show. They were asking if my wife and I would appear on the show, but we declined the offer.

We were again approached by the media and eventually, we replied to a journalist from the Sunday Telegraph magazine 'Seven.' After our interview, the article went to print and we were not happy with the result. We felt let down, as it did not get across well enough that Neil had not had a fair trial. In fact, she said at one point that Neil had eighteen credit cards, which was complete fiction, as this information never came out in trial.

We were totally disillusioned with the trial and the judge in particular, who ultimately oversees everything. I would go as far to say that once it had been realised that the gun shot residue forensic evidence on Rachel had been found to have been withheld, the trial should have been quashed. After all, on the stand, the Medical Examiner did admit that he would have wanted this evidence, had it been available to him. What else had been hidden from him? I wanted to share my feelings with the correct department over the pond and so, I wrote to the Governor of Massachusetts. We laid down before him our arguments on why we thought the trial judge had not allowed our son a fair trial and we received a reply.

Our reply came back from the Director of Western MA Governor's Office, who said on behalf of the Governor, "We are pleased that you contacted us with an issue of such gravity. However, the Governor has no role in issues relating to judicial conduct. To address your concerns, you must contact the Commission on Judicial Conduct."

Given that Neil's case, if it were successful at appeal level, would be granted a retrial before the same judge, I decided against submitting a complaint at this time, as the judge might hold it against us. When, eventually, we did contact the Commission on Judicial Conduct following the completion of the appeals process and where we laid before them what we thought were the irregularities within the trial, we received a swift reply from the Executive Director.

In the reply, it stated that the Commission has the powers to review the actions of the Massachusetts State Court judges when they constitute judicial misconduct. It stated, "Your submission appears to describe reasons why you disagree with the legal decisions made by the judge. Under Massachusetts General Laws, the Commission does not have the power to review a judge's legal decisions for error. Rules we follow state that in the absence of fraud, corrupt motive, bad faith, or a clear indication that the judge's conduct violates the code of judicial conduct, the commission shall not take action against a judge for making findings of fact, reaching a legal conclusion, or applying the law as she understands it. Commission proceedings shall not be a substitute for an appeal. As your complaint does not allege specific facts that, if true, would constitute judicial misconduct, we cannot docket or investigate this complaint."

We had in our possession a leaflet from our Foreign and Commonwealth Office, which stated that they would consider supporting a pardon or clemency pleas where there is evidence that seems to point to a miscarriage of justice. When questioned about this, they said that this was only possible once the appeals process is exhausted and then it could only be considered if the appeals lawyer proposed it. To this, I asked them to, please give me the evidence that this is indeed the case. In reply, the FCO admitted that they had made a mistake in what they had said. It is not mandatory for the lawyer to make the first move as previously stated, even though they would ask the lawyer for their view.

After much asking, the FCO said that we could meet them face to face at the Old Admiralty Building, The Mall, London. We were to meet two civil servants there who were the Desk Officers for the North America Country Casework Team. They were polite and seemed to be taking an interest in what points we were making, and to that extent, they were taking notes. I asked what they were going to do with the notes and I was told that they would be passed onto the Vice Consul in Boston, and so then I asked what this person would do with them. There was no reply to this question. Maybe it was a waste of time, but where are we supposed to go for any help? In our position, you will try anything.

The Appeals Process

It was the job of the trial defence lawyers to identify issues and to make any necessary objections to the trial judge's rulings, and then preserve them for the appellate review. Everything that was objected to in trial and which the judge overruled, could be presented on appeal by Neil's appeals lawyer.

Key issues challenged at the trial were; the two searches made of Neil's home by the police, which were classed by the trial and appeals lawyers as illegal; and the trial judge's part in jury selection process. It was stated by the lawyers for Neil that the judge's part in the jury selection process made this a charade. They stated that the judge believed that she was conducting a fair enquiry to perspective jurors and it's just her way of thinking that didn't allow for a more expansive approach. Her way of thinking seemed to be; "I am here, and I am going to show everybody that I can run it here. It will take as many days as it takes me, but I will get jurors who, when you read a transcript of voir dire, will seem perfect. But it wasn't perfect. It became a results-orientated exercise to get on paper a record that would muster. It was never an effort to obtain jurors who were genuinely free from bias or prejudice. And without that as a starting effort, the results were pre-ordained," said the defence lawyer.

The appeal could be fought on every error the judge or prosecutor made, from the denial of the motion to suppress, to the denial of the application for a change of venue, to the denial of the motion to re-prejudicial publicity. It was said by the defence lawyers, with regards to a change of trial venue, that when it comes to venue changes, you should start where the story has been most saturated and where the jury pool has been effected by and exposed to the publicity, and certainly, the ground zero for that was the Middlesex County. What we experienced during the trial process led us to believe that this was not the right venue. There was no way to know the extent of exposure to the public going beyond Middlesex County. The lawyers said our concern is that it is going to set a precedent. If this case does not qualify for moving it put out of ground zero, we don't know if there will ever be one.

There are two levels of appellate reviews, the first being the Supreme Judicial Court of Massachusetts and if there is a federal issue, then the appeal could go to the Federal Courts. In the first instance, nothing can be done until the entire transcripts from the trial have been completed and sent to go to the appeals lawyer.

In July 2011, the brief of the appeals lawyer was submitted to the Supreme Judicial Court judges. He challenged, firstly, the two searches by the police to Neil's home in Hopkinton. He stated that this violated the Fourth Amendment to the Federal Constitution as well as Article 14 of the Massachusetts Declaration of Rights. The purpose of the Fourth Amendment is to safeguard the privacy and security of individuals against arbitrary invasions of government officials. The trial judge, he said, ruled the two entries did not violate the Fourth Amendment or Article 14. This, he said, was incorrect as a matter of law.

Evidence, therefore, seized by the police and all derivative evidence subsequently obtained by the police as a result of the primary seizures, should have been suppressed under the Fourth Amendment. Also, the process of choosing the jury violated due process, and denied Neil his right to a fair and impartial jury guaranteed by the Fifth, Sixth and Fourteenth Amendments to the Federal Constitution and Article 12 of the Massachusetts Declaration of Rights. The lawyer stated that in the exercise of its extraordinary powers, this court should order a new trial.

In reply to this argument, the prosecution said that the police acted reasonably and within the confines of their caretaking role when conducting two wellbeing checks at the request of the family members. They said the victim's bodies would, in any event, have been eventually found.

Given that the police did not follow the correct search procedure meant that the crime scene was disturbed and contaminated.

The trial judge agreed with the prosecutors, who argued that the police were justified in entering the house (with civilians), and rejected the motion by Neil's trial lawyers. The trial judge wrote this in a twenty-two-page decision; "In these circumstances, I find that the entries into the Entwistle's home were reasonable and did not violate the Fourth Amendment prohibition against unreasonable searches and seizures."

Oral Argument and Result

The oral argument was held in front of the Supreme Judicial Court on the 17th April 2012. My wife and I volunteered to be at this session, but we were advised against it by Neil's appellate lawyer. This part of the process lasted forty minutes. Alongside the appellate lawyer were the two trial lawyers. It speaks volumes that these two very experienced and very busy trial lawyers were taking the time out to show a unified stance against this injustice taking place.

The appellate lawyer, on taking the lead, faced intense questioning at times by the five Supreme Judicial Court judges facing him. He said that the police did not have the appropriate warrants to enter the defendant's house to seize evidence and this evidence should have been suppressed. On the two occasions the police entered the house, they did not have objective knowledge that there was a person in the house in need of immediate aid. The inevitable discovery doctrine does not purge the taint on the evidence seized as a direct result of these unlawful searches. This court had to, very carefully, consider if it wanted to lower the standards of crossing that boundary of constitutionality.

The appeals lawyer also argued that the trial's international media coverage rose to extraordinary levels in Massachusetts history. There was also extraordinary, prejudicial pre-trial publicity in the case, that was both, saturating and inflammatory, and this cannot be legitimately disputed. He said that that the defendant is entitled to a new trial utilising a jury selection process where there can be no question that the seated jurors are fair and impartial.

The prosecutor argued that the police were not investigating a crime, rather they were in the house to make sure no one was there that was missed in the first search, or to find evidence of where they had gone.

Neil's trial lawyers said, following the court hearing, that the SJC had a chance to reverse bad rulings. If the court failed to rule against the decision made in trial, then he would take the case to the federal court level, all the way to the US Supreme Court. Neil would not automatically be eligible for our equivalent of legal aid.

Whilst Neil's appeal was in progress, a result was released from the same court house. The case was Commonwealth vs E. Toolan (SJC-10227), and it was concluded that flaws in the jury process required the reversal of the convictions of a man found guilty of first degree murder.

Immediately, I contacted Neil's trial and appellate lawyer's, to let them know that we were aware of this case, and each one of them replied to me to state that this news was in their eyes significant.

The Supreme Judicial Court had 130 days to make their decision in the case, but could ask for an extension on this. I was just as nervous waiting for this decision as I was in the trial. On the 15th August 2012, the decision came out. The judges upheld the verdict of the trial. This decision was given out on the last day and so was made to look as if the judges had taken the maximum time to consider their decision. This was a bitter pill to swallow for us all.

An unbelievable extract from the oral argument, between the appellate lawyer and the five judges was when the lawyer started to make his opening statement. He immediately refers to the Commonwealth's brief that involves the emergency aid doctrine. He stated that the Commonwealth argues that a reasonable, objective police officer could have concluded before the second search that the Entwistle family was still in the house, even though there is no factual basis for that on record and it is unfounded.

Immediately, a judge interjected by saying, "Does it matter, does it matter?"

Obviously, the prosecution again got away with saying things that were not true.

Later that year, the appellate lawyer was informed that he had received the funding from the Committee for Public Council Services to take the appeal to the next level, such was the respect the council had for him. By November, he had to submit a written argument to see if the Supreme Court would, in fact, allow the case to go forward.

The submission was submitted in plenty of time and we checked on the relevant web page that it had been received. It stated under the section Proceedings and Orders that a petition for a writ of certiorari and motion for leave to proceed, in forma pauperise, was filed. We had to ask the appellate lawyer what this meant. He replied that the prosecution can write a response to the petition, but that they are not obligated to unless ordered by the Court.

In the petition, it was asked whether the emergency aid exception to the search warrant requirement of the Fourth Amendment ever permits a second search of a home by the police, after the first search of the home fails to reveal any kind of an emergency taking place inside that home.

The Fourth Amendment to the United States Constitution states that the right of the people to be secure in their persons, houses, papers and effects, against unreasonable searches and seizures, shall not be violated, and no Warrants shall issue, but upon probable cause, supported by Oath or affirmation, and particularly describing the place to be searched, and the persons or things to be seized.

Even though the police officers unequivocally testified to entering the home a second time to look for any signs of the family's whereabouts, the Supreme Judicial Court substituted its own judgement for that of law enforcement. In fact, the Supreme Judicial Court never properly addressed the legal issue of whether the second search was justified, merely to look for evidence of the Entwistle's whereabouts.

The lawyer argued that the reason for granting this petition is that this case offers the Court the opportunity to clarify the important and what will undoubtedly become the reoccurring issue of whether a second search of a home is ever permissible under the emergency aid exception to the search warrant requirement under the Fourth Amendment, when the first search fails to reveal any kind of emergency taking place within the home.

The lawyer also explained that the emergency aid exception is an important part of this Court's Fourth Amendment jurisprudence. This case amply shows that the police and the lower courts need practical guidance on the reach of the emergency aid exception.

Fighting Back

While we were waiting for the outcome of the Supreme Court, we continually wrote to our government departments about the abuse of the law in Neil's case. In most cases, we received respectful replies to acknowledge our letters. One letter stands out above the others, the Shadow Foreign Secretary, Douglas Alexander, challenged the then Foreign Secretary, William Hague on the issues we had raised and asked that he be kept informed of the outcome. This lifted Neil's spirits somewhat, if only for a brief period. Nick Clegg MP and Harriet Harman MP sympathised with our difficulties too. The Shadow Home Secretary at the time, Yvette Cooper, answered to say that she was grateful to hear of our experiences, which she said would help to hold the government to account and develop policy in the future.

In January 2013, we received what I suppose we were expecting and that was the news that Neil had been unsuccessful in his attempt to get his case heard in the Supreme Court in Washington.

Neil was a victim of circumstances. Yes, he made mistakes in the way he behaved after he found the bodies, but I cannot say how I would have reacted on finding my family in the way he did and who could? We will never stop trying to overturn his conviction as there is so much wrong with the case.

In 2015, I became acquainted with a former detective, now a true-crime writer who has been published ten times, Duncan McNab. We have met several times, but on the first occasion, I met Duncan in London where we had a cup of coffee on Kings Cross station. On parting, Duncan said to me, how did we get connected and I stated it was through his Australian agent. I sent my original story over a large area to find someone who was interested.

Duncan has travelled to the US to meet Neil in prison. On the tenth anniversary of the case, I was contacted by an American newspaper and straight away I referred them to Duncan, who put the cat among the pigeons in what he said. This was someone who was qualified to have a just opinion and who was totally neutral in his stance.

Duncan's comments can be read in the MetroWest Daily News article of 17th January 2016, titled: 'True crime author sees holes in Entwistle murder case.' (Go to metrowestdailynews.com .)

In the article, Duncan said, "It's one of those bloody mysteries you can't put out of your mind," and "I keep seeing reasonable doubt." He goes onto say, "There's a plausible alternative scenario," and he concludes, "He might be guilty, but on the other hand, there's a strong possibility he is not."

As Neil's father, I have approached several organisations to try and get help to bring attention to Neil's case, but so far, I have been unsuccessful. I will not give up.

Afterword

I wish to speak about Neil and the sort of man I know him to be. Neil has several great qualities, but they are also the source of his greatest flaws. Neil will help anyone in need, be they friend, a stranger, or an enemy, regardless of the cost to himself; he gets this from me.

When Neil was seventeen, he was standing, one day, in the school yard waiting for a class when he saw a girl trying to escape from a crowd of twenty or so taunting bullies. In response, Neil made his way to the crowd and pushed his way through them to get to the girl. At first, she thought he was part of the crowd and pushed him away as he moved beside her, but he managed to reassure her. He put his arm around her shoulder and led her away, using his body as a shield. He never responded to the bullies, either in defence or attack; his motive was not to confront or to punish but simply to save the girl from harm. Eventually, the bullies gave up and left.

It is a significant fact to say that at no time throughout Neil's case has anyone ever said that they had even seen Neil get mad or frustrated, let alone violent. In fact, the opposite is true. Proudly, I can say to this day Neil remains as always, a gentle man.

Neil is also fiercely loyal in protecting the reputation of those who are close to him, even if it means others think the worst of him; he gets this from Yvonne. When Neil saw what Rachel had done, his desire was to protect Rachel's reputation from the stigma of infanticide and suicide. He similarly desired to save Joseph Matterazzo from knowing his gun had been used in such a terrible way. He tried to carry a burden that was too large for him and that was not his responsibility to bear. This was the start of Neil's undoing. The Matterazzo family have shown in plenty that they were not worthy of such loyalty.

In 2013, after all of Neil's avenues of appeal had been exhausted, Neil attempted to reach out to Rachel's mum and stepfather. When he wrote to Yvonne and me about it, we were against the idea. These people who have chosen to enjoy all the benefits the courts, the charities and others have given them as they've been treated as victims of Neil, even before his wrongful conviction. They have done this without ever reaching out to us with an acknowledgement of the loss we suffered with them. In a nut shell, we do not trust them.

Though he listened to us and considered what we had to say, Neil followed his conscience and attempted to reach out to them nonetheless. Neil cannot help but try to see the best in people. He approached the superintendent of the prison, a woman who believed everything that she had read in the press about him. She warned him in no uncertain terms that he was not to attempt to reach out on his own, which he already knew, but she did say she would make enquiries through the prison's victim outreach coordinator. She waited a further week to inform Neil that, in answer to his request to meet with them, the Matterazzo's said, "No, not at this time." Neil asked if he may write a letter to them and the following week he was told, no. Neil's concern is that the prison made these decision on their own without contacting the Matterazzo's. After all, they had denied Neil the opportunity of having an interview at the request of Piers Morgan. In Neil's case, every door is closed to anything that they think would benefit him and there has been a vendetta against him from the very beginning.

I wish to share with you the letter Neil proposed to send to them.

April 2013

Dear Priscilla,

I want you to know that the following words have been written with love and compassion, that they are words of regret and remorse, and that I hope through them, we may start to pursue peace between us.

For over seven years, I have never shared what I saw and what I know of all that transpired on the day that we both lost Rachel and Lilly, the two most wonderful people ever to bless our lives. At first, my silence was borne out of a desire to protect Rachel's memory, and to save you and Joe from further hurt. Obviously, that did not work out as I had hoped. After I was arrested, my silence was prompted by the advice of my lawyers and so it has been until now.

Now that my appeals have been exhausted, now that my conviction is final and now that I must face the many tens of years of my natural life in prison, I know I must clear my conscience by sharing all that I have, until now, kept to myself. As strange as it sounds, my failed trial and appeal, though denying me the physical freedom for which I had hoped, have left me free to share this great burden I have carried in my heart. I hope that we both will be blessed with greater closure and peace through this.

I must warn you that what I have to share will be very difficult for you to hear, as it will be for me to say. Because of this, I want to reassure you that I will speak nothing but love and compassion, regret and remorse, and with a full acknowledgement of all the ways that I failed as a husband, as a father, as a son, and as a son-in-law. I did not kill Rachel and Lilly, but I do carry the guilt and in no way blame Rachel. And this is where it is difficult for me to share openly.

In order to share all that transpired, it will be necessary for me to share Rachel's part in it all. Rachel was my wife and I loved her more than I loved anyone else, even Lilly. She could do no wrong in my eyes, so I want you to know that even with difficult things I have to share, you will hear neither judgment nor accusation in my tone because I hold none against her and I never have.

I probably need no more than fifteen minutes to share the crux of what is on my heart, though I could speak for hours. I would also like to offer you as much time as you may wish to speak or vent openly, freely and without fear of interruption from me, if this is something you may want. I also wish to offer you the chance to bring with you any number of people for support, be it family and friends, or even the District Attorney and such, if you wish.

I do hope you can find the compassion and strength to meet with me, but I fully understand if you cannot. Every time I see you on TV, I yearn to reach out to you, but there is such a great barrier between us. Whether or not you decide to allow me to share with you all that I know, please know that I still love you and care about you, and that I pray daily for you to receive the immense comfort we both need, having lost Rachel and Lilly.

With love,

Neil.

We still think that Neil made the wrong decision in attempting to reach out to them, but that's who Neil is.

Finally, let me say this: Neil should not be spending his life in prison for something he did not do; he should not be spending his life in prison for reacting badly to a traumatic event he beheld that fateful day. We will never stop speaking out against the injustices done; we will never stop fighting for justice for our innocent son.

CPSIA information can be obtained
at www.ICGtesting.com
Printed in the USA
BVHW09s1114011018
528932BV00033B/2848/P

The Neil Entwistle murder case caused a media frenzy on both sides of the Atlantic. With his wife and baby daughter found dead in their bedroom, Neil was the immediate suspect, and his subsequent conviction seemed inevitable to all who heard and read the sordid coverage. However, things are not always what they seem.

With remarkable objectivity, Cliff Entwistle reveals the inconsistencies in the investigation, the lies told and the key forensic evidence withheld from the medical examiner, and with touchingly personal candour, he shares the pain he felt at the great loss and betrayal his family suffered.

You will be disturbed by the harrowing details he exposes of the justice systems of both the UK and the US, yet you cannot fail to be encouraged as he testifies to the strength and resilience of family bonds in the face of unimaginable heartache and adversity.

www.austinmacauley.com

US$6.95 / C$8.95
£7.99 / AUS$12.95 / NZ$13.95

9 781528 900577

AUSTIN MACAULEY PUBLISHERS™
LONDON · CAMBRIDGE · NEW YORK · SHARJAH